The Turf

Three Centuries of
Horse Racing

The Turf

Three Centuries of Horse Racing

Roger Longrigg

Eyre Methuen
London

Picture Credits

Acknowledgements and thanks for permission to reproduce pictures are due to The Radio Times Hulton Picture Library for plates 2 to 7, 9, 10, 12 to 15, 17, 19 to 21, 23, 25 to 33, 35 to 45, 47, 50 to 58, 62, 63, 66, 67, 71 to 73, 79 to 81, 84, 85, 91, 92, 94, 98 to 114, 116 to 120, 123 to 131, 134, 136, 138 to 141, 143 to 145, and 147 to 150; to the Illustrated London News & Sketch Ltd for plates 22, 24, 46, 48, 49, 59, 60, 68, 69, 82, 93, 95, 115, 121, 122, and 142; to Sport & General Press Agency for plates 16, 18, 96 and 97; to the Racing Information Bureau for plate 74; and to the National Portrait Gallery for plate 135. No copyright has been wittingly infringed in any picture reproduced in this book.

The pictures on the front and back of the jacket are reproduced by kind permission of Mrs Harry Middleton and The British Museum respectively.

Grateful thanks are due to Miss Thelma Schaverien for the picture research throughout.

PICTUREFILE

First published 1975
by Eyre Methuen Ltd
11 New Fetter Lane, EC4P 4EE
© 1975 Roger Longrigg
Printed in Great Britain by
Butler & Tanner Ltd
Frome and London

ISBN 413 32960 7

Contents

Under Starter's Orders

Horse racing has an enormous library of history, memoir, treatise and fiction, tons of official record, mountains of journalistic description. It used to be painted almost weekly, and is now photographed many times daily. At every moment its stage has been crowded with great or peculiar horses and great or peculiar men. Its history is full of changing conditions, developing law, proliferating villainy, of a few fortunes won and many lost; the hero of the whole story is the English thoroughbred, most magnificent of mongrels, without whose courage and brilliance no one would cross the street to see the Derby. The following pages are a personal selection, from all this richness, intended to add up to a fair account of how modern racing came to be the glorious sport and great industry that it is.

1. Horses

Modern racing depended on the
creation of the racehorse, which was
achieved by selective breeding and by
the use of Eastern stallions (1). The
value of this exotic blood lay in the
toughness, stamina and docility of the
desert horses, and in the fact that, after
centuries of careful line breeding, they
were genetically prepotent. They were
small, but selective breeding increased
the height of their descendants by
about an inch every 25 years.
Thoroughbreds are not pure Arabs:
but some, like the Aga Khan's little
grey Mahmoud, Derby winner of 1936
(2), look very like it.

3

5

From three imported stallions descend all modern thoroughbreds in tail male. The oldest was a miscalled Turk captured at Buda in 1688 (4); he was ridden as a charger by Captain Byerley, then went to stud in England. The second was bought by Thomas Darley in Aleppo in 1704 and sent home to Yorkshire (3). He got among others Flying Childers (6), of unprecedented racing excellence. The effect of his brilliance was more importation; this included a Yemeni stallion miscalled a Barb (5), who went to the Earl of Godolphin's stud: he there depended for tranquility on the company of the cat Grimalkin.

7

9

Flying Childers's full brother had a great-grandson, foaled in 1764, called Eclipse (9, 10); he belonged to Dennis O'Kelly, once the front legs of a sedan chair. He was the best racehorse of his time by a devastating margin, and the reason why the Darley Arabian is the tail-male ancestor of the great majority of today's thoroughbreds. Contributing to this result were the Byerley Turk's descendants Herod and his son Highflyer, with many of whose mares Eclipse was bred. Typical of Eclipse's sons was O'Kelly's Dungannon (7), out of a Herod mare, who loved his sheep as the Godolphin Arabian loved Grimalkin.

Eclipse's most important son was Pot-8-os (originally Potatoes, then Potooooooooo): his Waxy, and his Whalebone. These two were both bred like Dungannon; both won the infant Derby while Eclipse ran in four-mile heat races. Whalebone's grandson Touchstone (8) dramatizes the main reason for this large and rapid change in the thoroughbred—he got 343 winners of 738 races worth nearly a quarter of a million pounds.

11

12

Other typical descendants of Whalebone were Blair Athol (12) and Hermit (11), winners of the Derbys of 1864 and 1867. The latter, Touchstone's grandson, caused the ruin and speeded the death of the hapless Marquess of Hastings.

From Hermit's sire Newminster descended Hyperion (13), a brilliant, lazy horse who won the Derby of 1933. One of his many great sons was Her Majesty the Queen's Aureole, beaten in the Derby of 1953 (14) by Pinza, a descendant of Blair Athol's sire Stockwell 'the Emperor of stallions'. By a not unusual chance, the superior racehorse was an inferior sire.

From Stockwell also descends Blue
Peter, who won the 1939 Derby (17).
The war prevented his meeting the
other star of Europe in the St Leger,
the French Pharis by Nearco's sire
Pharos, of the same male line. The
immortal Nearco was bred in Italy;
many of his best descendants are
American; which shows how
international it had all become.
Bred like Nearco by Frederico Tesio,
Donatello II descended from
Stockwell's Irish grandsire
Birdcatcher, grandson of Whalebone.
Donatello's sons include Alycidon,
Ascot Gold Cup 1949 (15), called the
last great stayer: supreme
thoroughbreds are no longer expected
to stay more than two miles.
Nearco's American great-grandsons
include Nijinsky (16) and Mill Reef
(18), Derbys of 1970 and 1971; these
two are evidence of the tremendous
quality of the American
thoroughbred, but also of the enduring
merit of this essentially English
bloodline.

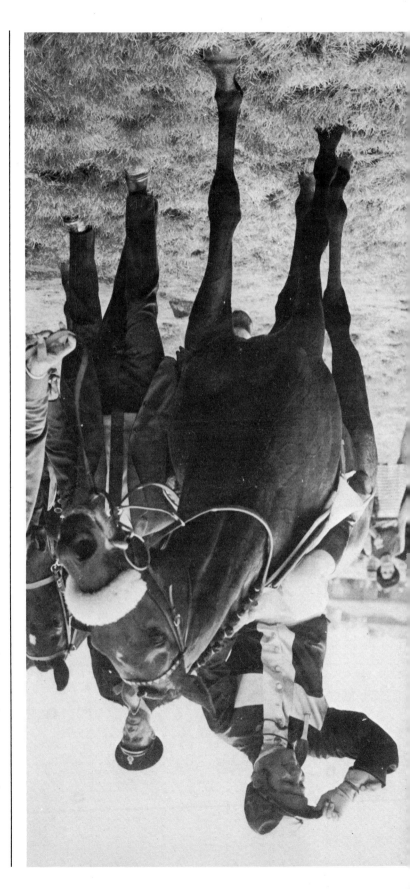

Hambletonian.

Another son of Eclipse of abiding importance was King Fergus. His son Hambletonian (20), out of a daughter of Highflyer, won in 1799 one of the most sensational matches in racing history. Hambletonian's great-great-grand son Voltigeur (19) lost in 1851 an even more celebrated match. From Voltigeur descended St Simon, the greatest racehorse of the late 19th century and perhaps the greatest sire in history.

The Byerley Turk-Herod male line is numerically far smaller, but it produced supreme horses in Bay Middleton and his son The Flying Dutchman (21), Voltigeur's conqueror in the 1851 match. His son Dollar was one of the most important stallions in French history.

Another descendant of Herod was Thormanby (22, left); his career illustrates, like Touchstone's, the change in the thoroughbred since the days of Eclipse; Thormanby ran 14 times as a two-year-old before winning the 1860 Derby.

OAKS.

BUTTERFLY.

The Godolphin Arabian's male line, through Matchem, is less numerous still. It survives today in the lines of Man O' War in America and Hurry On in Europe. Hurry On's sons included Coronach, winner of the 1926 Derby and St Leger (23).

Through these centuries, if racing needed breeders, breeders needed racing, as it provided the one valid test. But the hazards are shown by Blue Gown (25) and Pretender (24), winners of the 1868 and 1869 Derbys: good horses, and abject failures at stud.

Another enduring drawback of the 'racecourse test' is illustrated by Brown Jack (26), perhaps the best-loved horse in turf history: his stamina and honesty were lost to posterity because he was a gelding.

27

28

2.Courses

Early racing needed racehorses; it did not financially need a public, or cater for its comfort. At Newmarket (27) the only way to enjoy racing was on horseback, though this little town became 'headquarters' in James I's reign. The keenest racegoers galloped in with the finishing horses (28); the Jockey Club forbade, but did not prevent, this inspiriting custom.

29

Hornpipe *leaping over* Pepperpot *his Rider and the Farmers Son at* Lincoln Races *Friday the 8th Sept.r 1797 —*

The public was not even kept off the course by rails, until James I suggested this device at Lincoln; but two centuries later persons still rushed out in front of the horses (29), and three centuries later the rails at Epsom did not deter the suffragette Emily Davison from killing herself under the king's Anmer in the 1913 Derby (30).

Epsom became popular in the 17th century and important in the 18th: but the finish of the 1791 Derby (32) shows how people watched the races. The Epsom Grandstand Association was not formed until 1828, and then it was controlled by rogues. The stand was very fine by the time Bay Middleton won the Derby of 1836 (31).

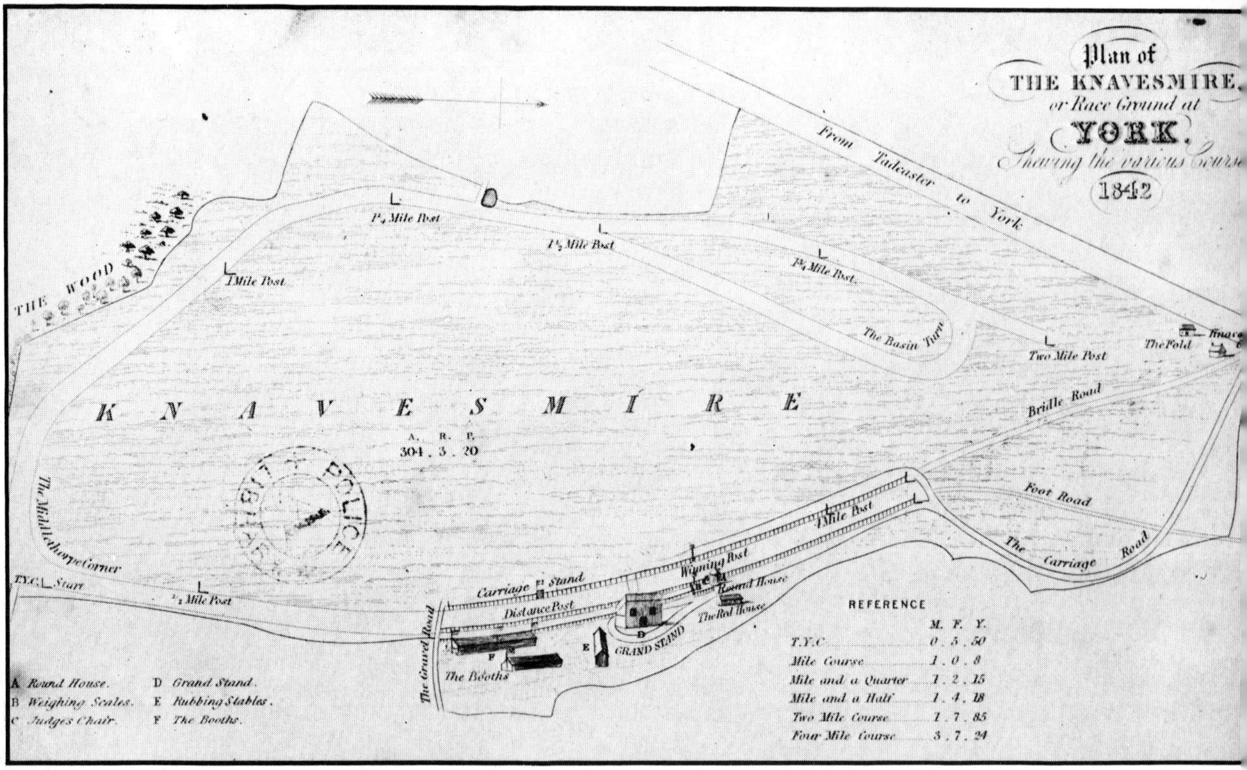
Plan of
THE KNAVESMIRE,
or Race Ground at
YORK,
Shewing the various Course
1842
From Tadcaster to York
THE WOOD
1 Mile Post
The Basin Turn
Two Mile Post
The Fold
K N A V E S M I R E
A. R. P.
304 . 3 . 20
Bridle Road
Foot Road
The Carriage Road
The Middlethorpe Corner
T.Y.C. Start
Carriage Stand
Distance Post
Winning Post
Round House
The Rail House
GRAND STAND
The Gravel Road
The Booths
A Round House.
B Weighing Scales.
C Judges Chair.
D Grand Stand.
E Rubbing Stables.
F The Booths.
REFERENCE
M. F. Y.
T.Y.C. 0 . 5 . 50
Mile Course 1 . 0 . 8
Mile and a Quarter 1 . 2 . 15
Mile and a Half 1 . 4 . 18
Two Mile Course 1 . 7 . 85
Four Mile Course 3 . 7 . 24

33

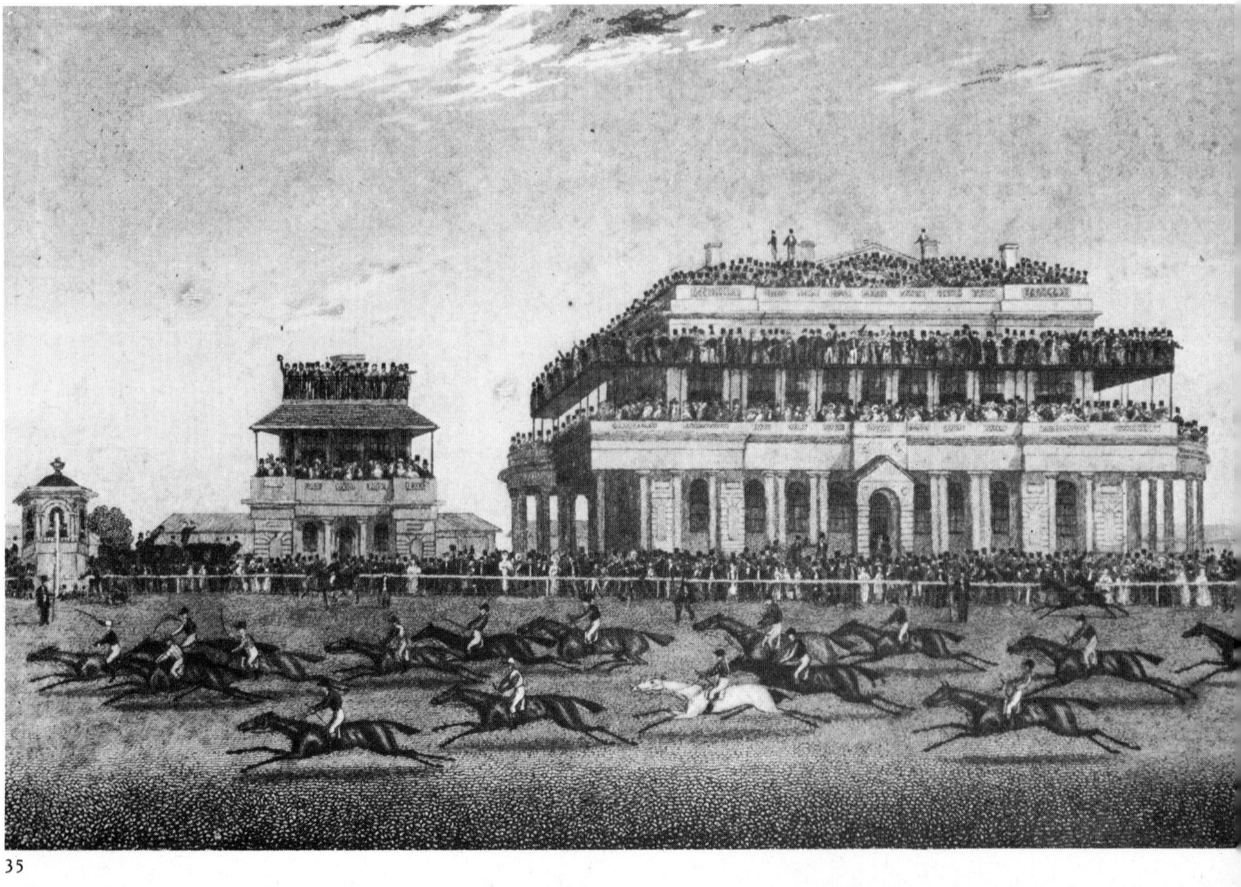

35

The leading northern courses had grandstands before those of the south. Doncaster's (35) was built by the Corporation on its new Town Moor course in 1776; the smaller stand to the left became successively a girls' school, a boys' school, and the County School for Deaf and Dumb Children. York's Knavesmire course (33) was the other principal one in the North, dating from 1709. Typically its small grandstand (36) was supplemented by booths, provided by the principal public houses of the city, and by a 'carriage stand' on the opposite side of the course.

Newcastle was one of many 'country courses' without the Gold Cups, Royal Plates or classic races of the major places mentioned. Its grandstand (34) doubled as an hotel, and held very few people. The rest wandered about on the raceground, a state of affairs which lasted until a new, enclosed course was laid out in 1881.

Country courses still humbler put on an immense amount of uncouth racing (37) between about 1680 and 1740, when there was an 'Act to restrain and prevent the Excessive Increase of Horse Races'. But after a

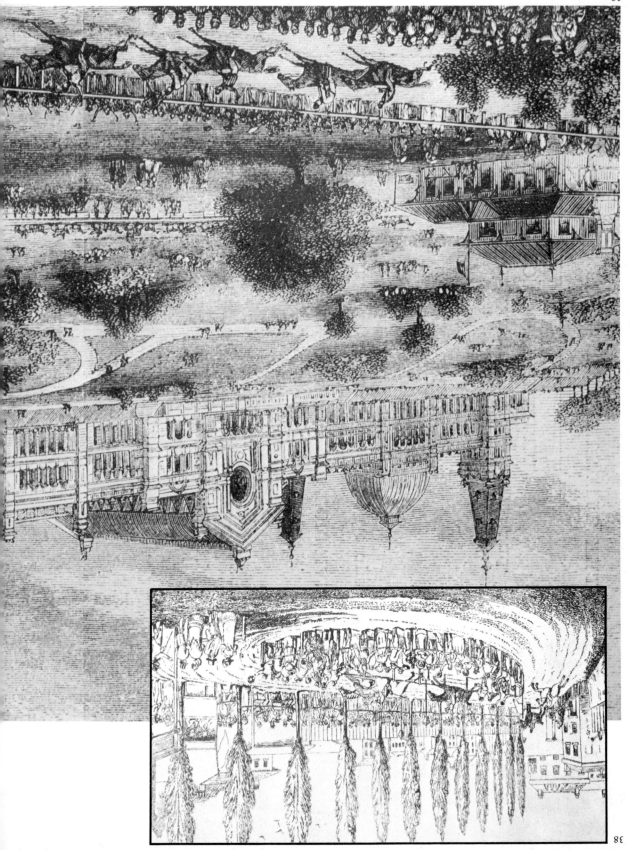

stable period, there was again a wild
growth of village and suburban racing
in the early 19th century, in places as
improbable as Kentish Town,
Bayswater and Sadlers Wells (38).
Alexandra Park – 'Ally Pally' to
generations of Londoners (39) – was
more respectable, but in atmosphere
remained, until its recent demise,
much more like Sadlers Wells than
like York or Newmarket.

40

Newmarket racecourse was owned by the Jockey Club. Almost all others were owned by Municipal Corporations, an idea invented in Chester in Henry VIII's reign. There were two special cases. One was Ascot, started by Queen Anne on her own property. Racing there was limited to hunters ridden to the Royal Buckhounds until the Duke of Cumberland (breeder of Herod and Eclipse) introduced orthodox events; a conventional grandstand followed (40). Ascot became more royal than ever when George IV initiated the Royal Procession, a stately precedent followed by every monarch, including George V (41).

41

A 'carriage stand' was still needed
(42), not only to accommodate
numbers, but also because vouchers to
the Royal Enclosure were not issued
to persons blemished by such stigmata
as divorce.

43

44

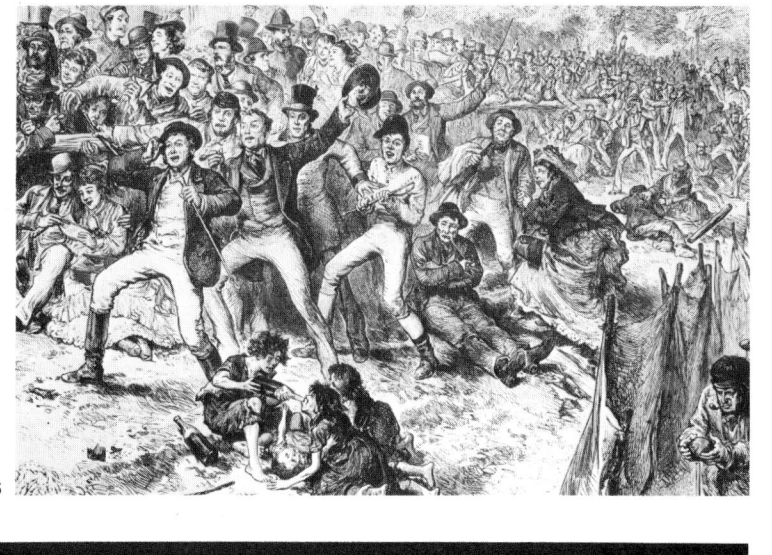

45

Another special case was
Goodwood (43), established by the
Duke of Richmond in his own park
and subject to his own rules. Park and
rules combined to create a
garden-party atmosphere (44), again
and again contrasted to the 'obscene
Bohemianism' of places like Epsom.
But people see what they want to see :
the drawing called 'Here They Come'
(45) is of Goodwood in 1875.

EPSOM.
DERBY DAY
18 44

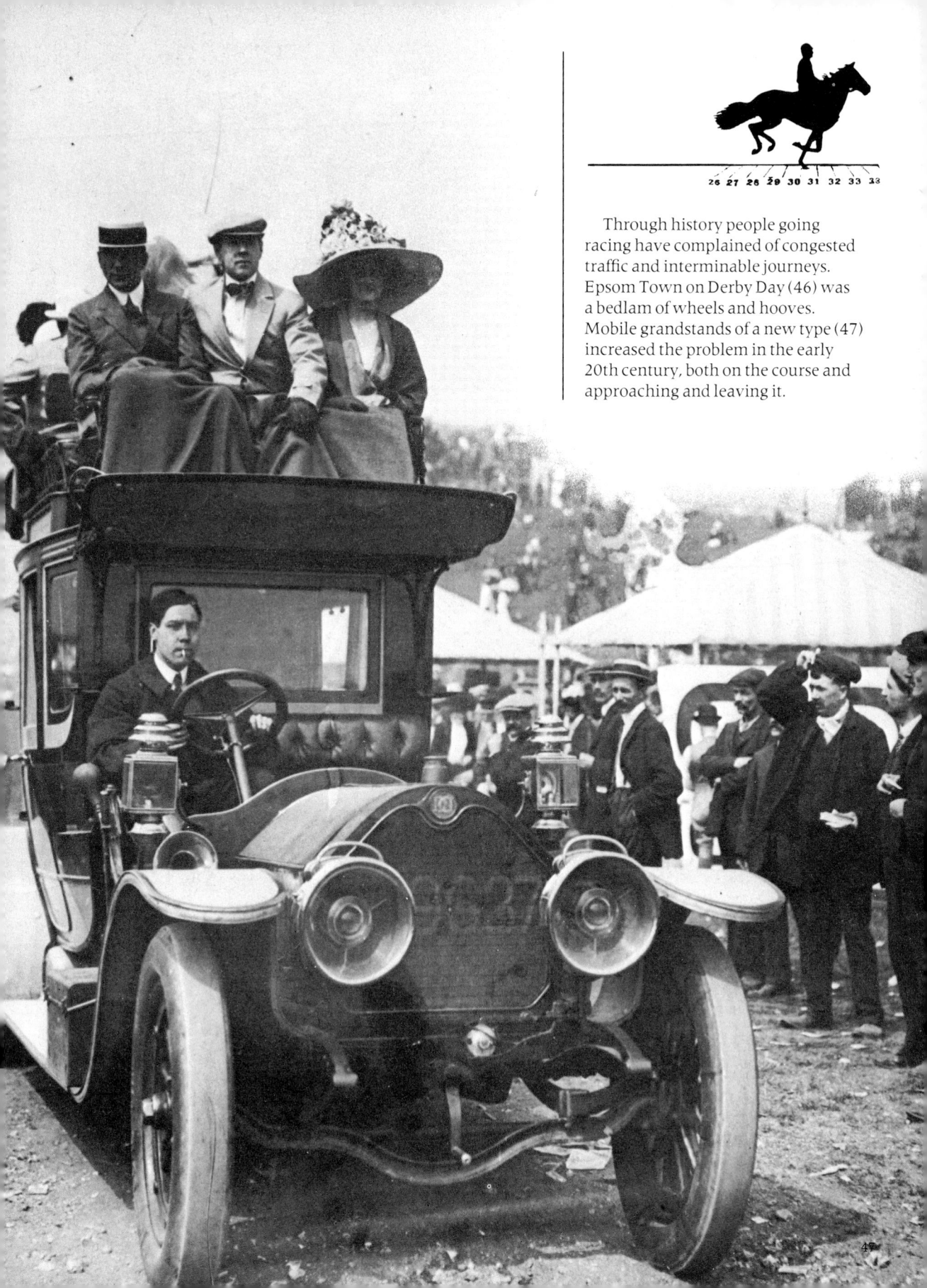

26 27 28 29 30 31 32 33 13

Through history people going racing have complained of congested traffic and interminable journeys. Epsom Town on Derby Day (46) was a bedlam of wheels and hooves. Mobile grandstands of a new type (47) increased the problem in the early 20th century, both on the course and approaching and leaving it.

47

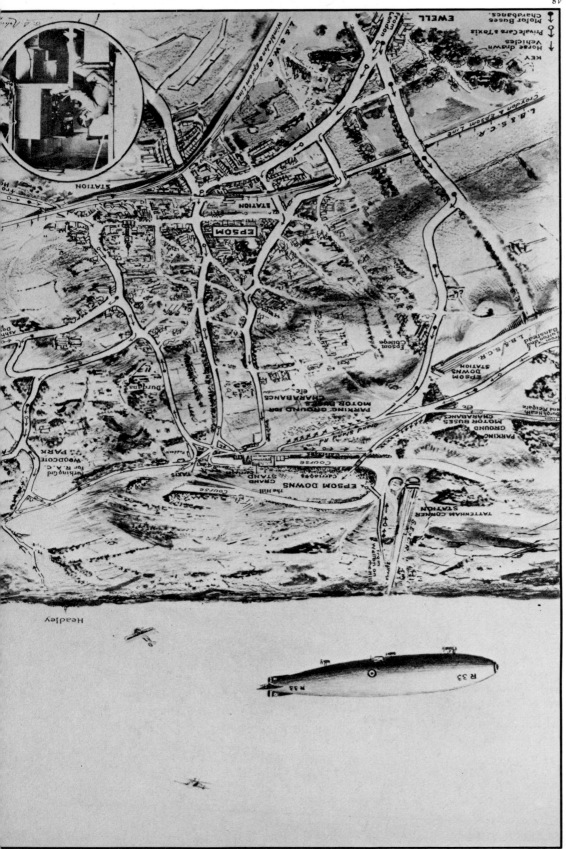

48

The 'carriage stand', when motorised, became even more capacious than the Grandstand (50), and these ponderous vehicles jammed the roads of southern England. In 1921 radio control, an airship, and an R.A.F. squadron were called in to control the traffic (48). But Epsom on Derby Day has always had special problems, including a traditional army of Gypsies (49) who read, and make, fortunes.

Many of the younger courses, like Kempton Park and Newbury, included their own railway stations among their amenities; this was impossible at Ascot, but the train and a short country walk (51) were, and are, often preferred to the miseries of the road.

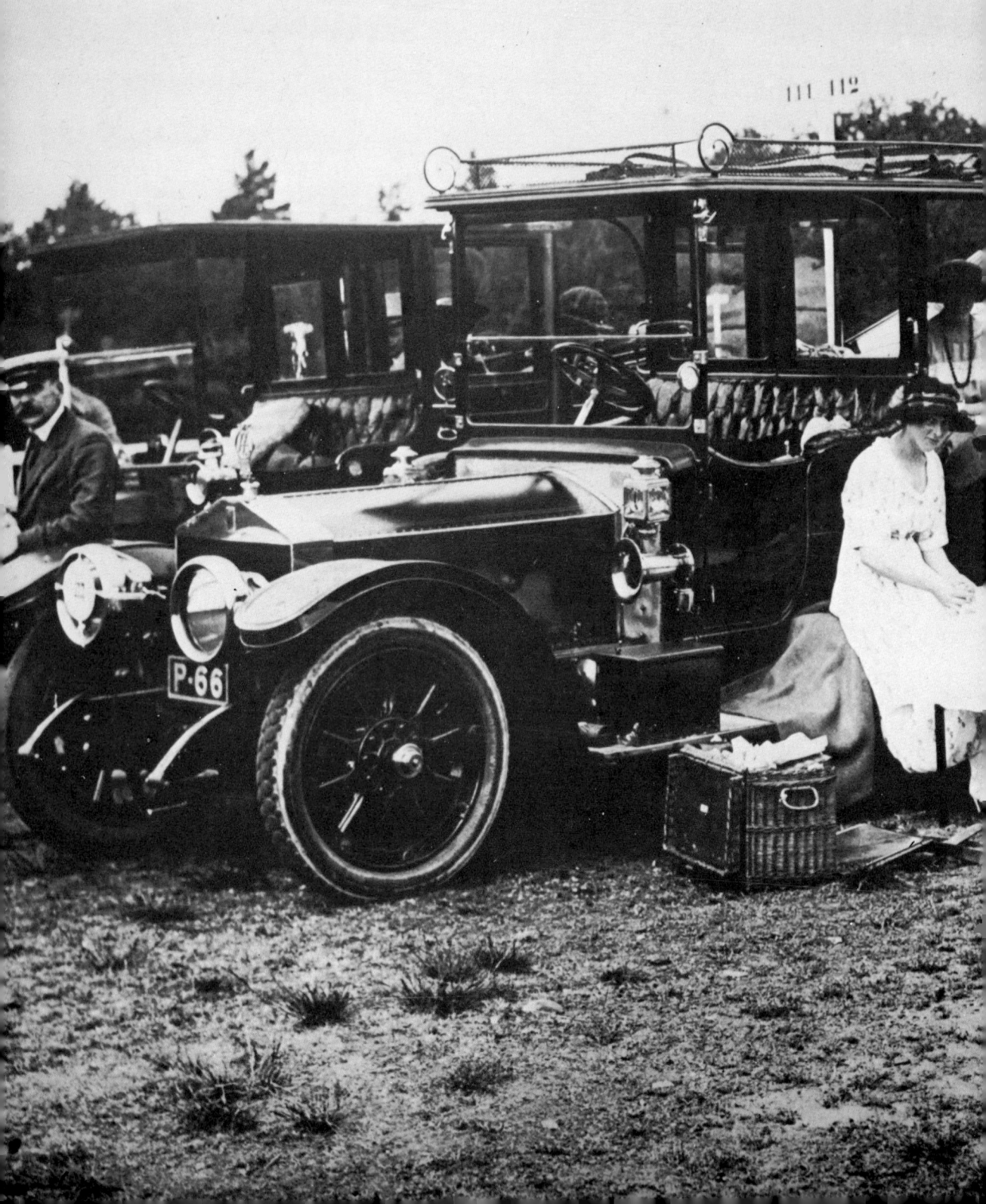

Racecourse catering developed from the convivial booths of the 18th century to the splendid dining-saloons of Victorian grandstands; a marked deterioration has been noticed since then. At Ascot (52) and Goodwood the picnic has flourished.

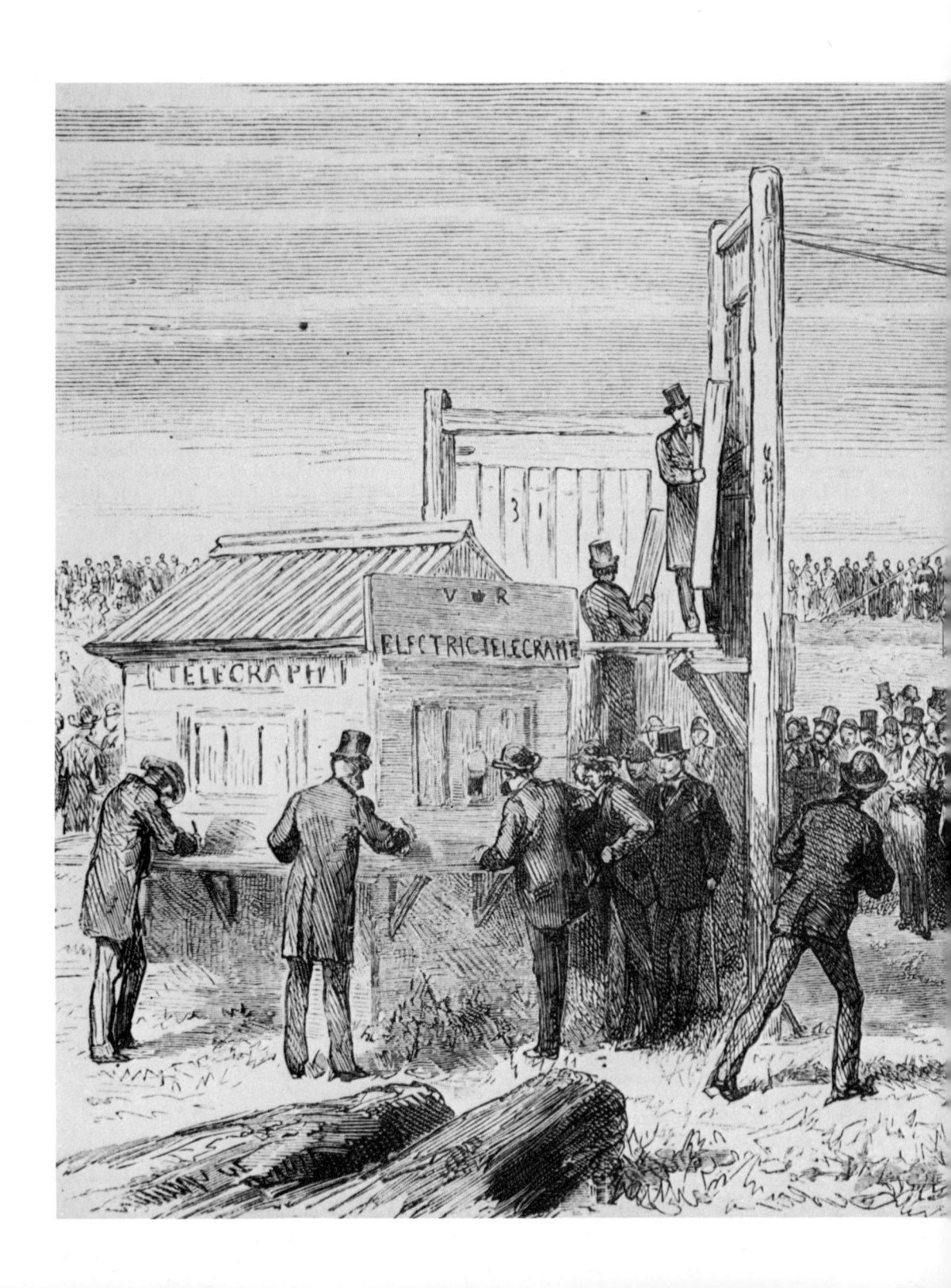

The greatest inconvenience suffered by the public was ignorance of which horse was which and what was running. Goodwood invented number-cloths in the 1840s, and the 'scratching board', copied from Australia, at last alerted punters not to back non-runners (53).

3. Races

In Charles II's early years most races were matches between two horses, both at Newmarket for prodigious wagers and in country places (54) for a sack of oats or a cow. The king specifically encouraged fields of horses to race against each other by offering substantial prizes; the first was his Town Plate at Newmarket, but cups, plates and purses followed even at little meetings like Dorsett Ferry, near Windsor (56). Matches survived as individual challenges outside the normal racing programme; some resulted from violent personal animosity, like that which animated the gallant but notorious 'Mrs Thornton' at York in 1804 (55).

CHESTER May 2ᵈ 1791.

S. Barry Esqᵉ's Bergamot 1 1 B.F. 2 2 B.C. Dis. B.F. Dis.

l. Ratcliffe's Mousetrap 4 1 1 Primrose 1 2 2 Needle 2 3 3
das 3 5 4 Ch.F. 5 4 Dr. B.C. Dr.

Mᵉ Fowler's Windlestone 1 1 Charlotte 2 2 B.H. 3 5 Citizen Dr. Harlot Dr.

Mᵉ Fowler's Windlestone 1 1 C.H. 4 2 Labourer 2 6 Laurel 3 4
itizen 5 3 Harlot Dr. Bywell Dr.

Col. Ratcliffe's Mousetrap 1 1 Gillyflower 3 2 Bergamot 2 Dr Drone 4 Dis
Windlestone Dr. B.C. Dr. B.F. Dr. B.M. Dr. Twilight Dr.

Hunters Race for a 100 Guineas.

oungo Noble Esqᵉ's School Boy 1 Trojan 2 B H 3 Lofty 4

homas Cholmondeley
and   Stewards
ohn Griffith Lewis Esqʳˢ

To whom this Plate is
Most Humbly Inscribed
by T. Hunter, Junʳ CHESTER

57

From the 1670s until about 1780 the important races were run in heats, usually four of four miles each; in the half hours between heats the runners were rubbed down (58) and the jockeys weighed in and out. A race in heats took all day; Chester's 1791 meeting (one of the six most important in England) had six races in a week, attracting only 20 horses in all (57).

The change from heat to dash racing happened quite quickly, both caused by and causing an immense change in the thoroughbred.

The first important 'dash' was a two-mile race for three-year-olds at Doncaster in 1776, which became the $1\frac{3}{4}$-mile St Leger. Long before the filly Apology won in 1874 (59) such 'classic' races had become the supreme ones.

The 12th Earl of Derby (61) and his friends devised a similar sweepstakes for fillies in 1779 at Epsom, named for his house The Oaks, and the year after a 1½-mile race for colts named for himself. By the time the Prince of Wales (Edward VII) won with Persimmon in 1896 (60), the Derby had been the turf's 'blue ribbon' for a century.

61

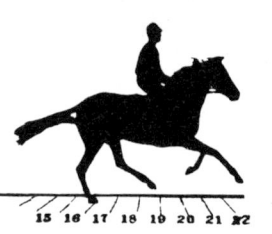

In contrast to the St Leger, it is run on a tricky course with a steep hill and a sharp bend (62)—an entirely different but equally valid test of the thoroughbred.

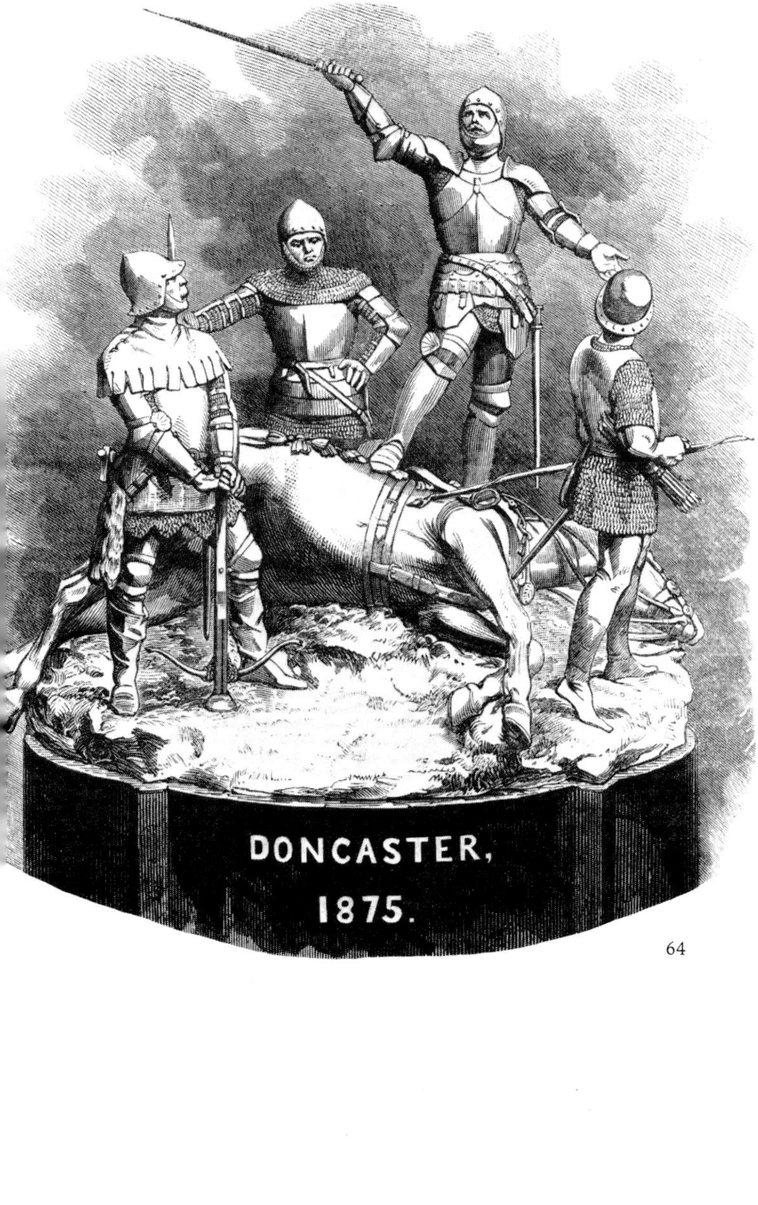

Newmarket followed Doncaster and Epsom with the two other classics: the 2000 Guineas in 1809 and the 1000 in 1814, both over only a mile. Winners of the Guineas, like Bahram in 1935 (63), sometimes go on to win the Derby: but many fail to stay $1\frac{1}{2}$ miles, and some become the sires of pure sprinters.

With the classics, the most important races were the Cups—over longer distances, and at weight for age—the trophies for which inspired Victorian craftsmen to prodigies of invention (64).

DONCASTER,
1875.

64

THE QUEEN'S GOLD CUP.	THE ASCOT CUP	THE ROYAL HUNT CUP.

65

67

Better spectacle and more open betting were achieved by the invention of handicaps. The first for more than two horses was the Oatlands Stakes at Ascot in 1791 (67); it was won by Baronet (66), ridden by the supreme and supremely dishonest Sam Chifney, and owned by the Prince of Wales (George IV). Top handicaps like the Royal Hunt Cup at Ascot merited trophies as resplendent as those for cup races (65), and winners were often of classic standard.

There was also a need for opportunities for the indifferent horses of humbler owners, which was filled by selling and claiming races. 'Sellers', after which the winner is auctioned on the course (68) remain a necessary part of the racing mix.

69

70

At every level, good races depended on fair starts. Originally a man said 'Go', which was often unsatisfactory. The flag start (70) was invented by Lord George Bentinck at Doncaster; it was an immense improvement. But with large fields, as in the Derby of 1864 (69), it was still grossly inadequate–it sometimes took more than an hour, and enabled favourites to be hopelessly impeded. A partial solution–by no means infallible–was to use as starter a person of tremendous authority, such as King Edward VII's racing manager Lord Marcus Beresford (71).

The long-established Australian method was at last brought to England, but was not without its own hazards (72).

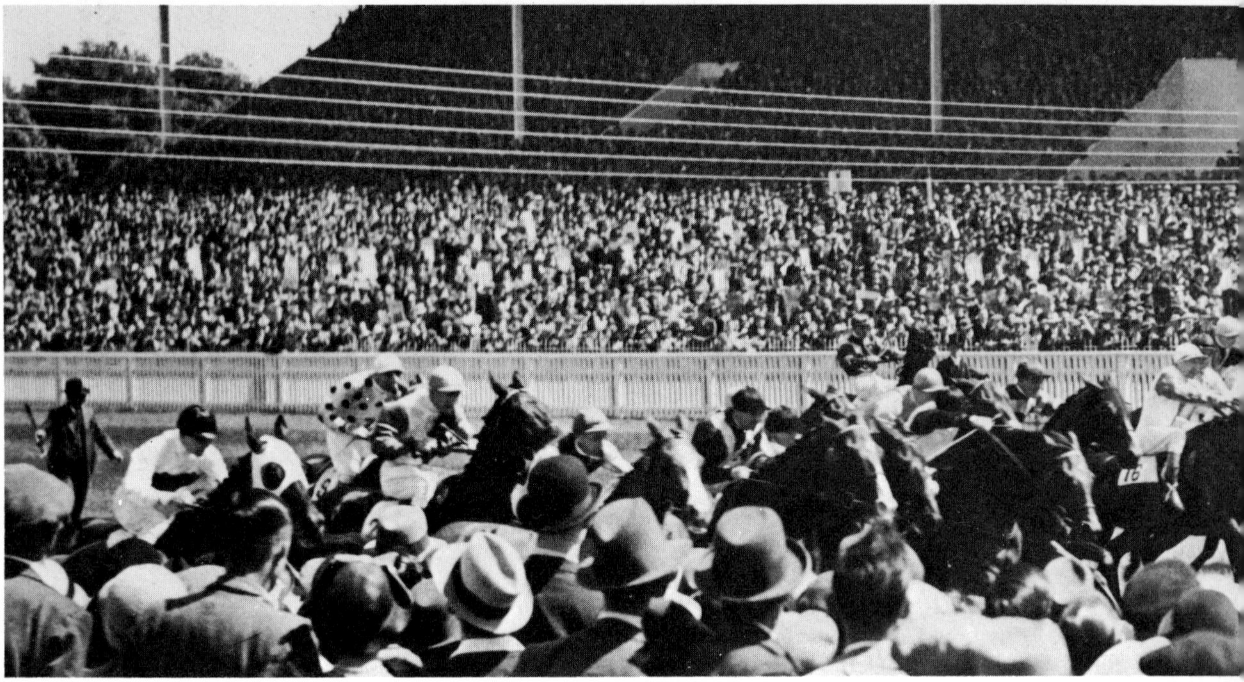

73

74

The multi-strand gate of some years later was an altogether safer device (73). But fair starts, as nearly guaranteed as possible, had to wait until the Jockey Club adopted the ugly and cumbersome stalls (74), invented long before in America and already invariable in all other leading racing countries.

75

77

76

4.Chases

Racing across country originally took the form of the 'wild goose chase' or 'pounding match', a sort of desperate follow-my-leader. In the late 18th century gentlemen rode matches from landmark to landmark (hence 'steeplechase'), which began to turn into races before 1800. The Grand Leicestershire Steeplechase was the best known of such events. Dick Christian, on the grey Magic in 1829 (75), was one of the few professional riders; most were amateurs, of whom the greatest was George Osbaldeston, the 'Squire' (76), master of the Quorn and Pytchley.

Steeplechasing was transformed in 1830 when Thomas Coleman, landlord of the Turf Hotel at St Albans, established a steeplechase on a round, well-marked course for the benefit of spectators, never before considered (77). This revolutionary idea was the more successful thanks to the participation of such dashing and glamorous amateurs as Lord Clanricarde (78), as well as professionals like Captain Becher.

78

There was immediate and enormous growth, notably at Cheltenham, the Vale of Aylesbury and Aintree. A steeplechase was first run at the last in 1836; the race considered the first Grand National in 1839 (79), during which Captain Becher christened, by immersion, one of the two brooks.

23 24 25 26 27 28 29 30 31

The winner was Lottery, ridden by Jem Mason (80). Mason was one of the very great jump jockeys of all time; Lottery was so pre-eminent that he occasioned the invention of handicap steeplechases.

81

83

The three steeplechase meetings of
1832 grew to 66 in 1842 ; these
included such forgotten fixtures as
Woolwich and Eltham (81). There was
comparable if smaller-scale growth in
Ireland. The great Irish steeplechasing
festival was Punchestown (83), which
started as the private meeting of the
Kildare hunt. A consequence was the
specialised development of the Irish
half-bred 'chaser ; a magnificent
example was Abd-el-Kader (84)
whose dam pulled a fast coach and
who was the first double winner of the
National (1850 and 1851).

Hurdle racing developed later and
more slowly ; the first hurdle race was
at Bristol in 1821 ; hurdling was part
of the programme at St Albans in the
1830s and at Northampton in
1844 (82).

Although steeplechasing was the child of foxhunting, hunt racing was entirely separate and usually on the flat–the Great Northamptonshire Stakes of 1844 (87) was part of the Pytchley Hunt Meeting. Meanwhile amateur jockeys, known, often generously, as Gentlemen Riders, deteriorated into much-mocked ineptitude after the great days of Osbaldestone and Clanricarde (85). At the same time the fences in professional steeplechases dwindled into paltriness in order that larger fields would be attracted. In dismay at these trends, Dr Fothergill Rowlands (86) organised an amateur National Hunt Steeplechase in 1859, from which grew not only a great renaissance but also the sport's governing body, the National Hunt Committee.

89

One result was a period dominated by amateurs. Among the greatest were George Ede, Mr Edwards (88), who won the National in 1868 and died after a fall in 1870, and Roddy Owen (89), who won the National in 1892 and died serving in Africa in 1895. An even more important result was the cleaning up of a pretty dirty sport and its proper administration. Tommy Pickernell (90)—himself one of the great Gentlemen Riders, riding in 17 Nationals and winning three—became in 1884 the National Hunt Committee's first Inspector of Courses.

90

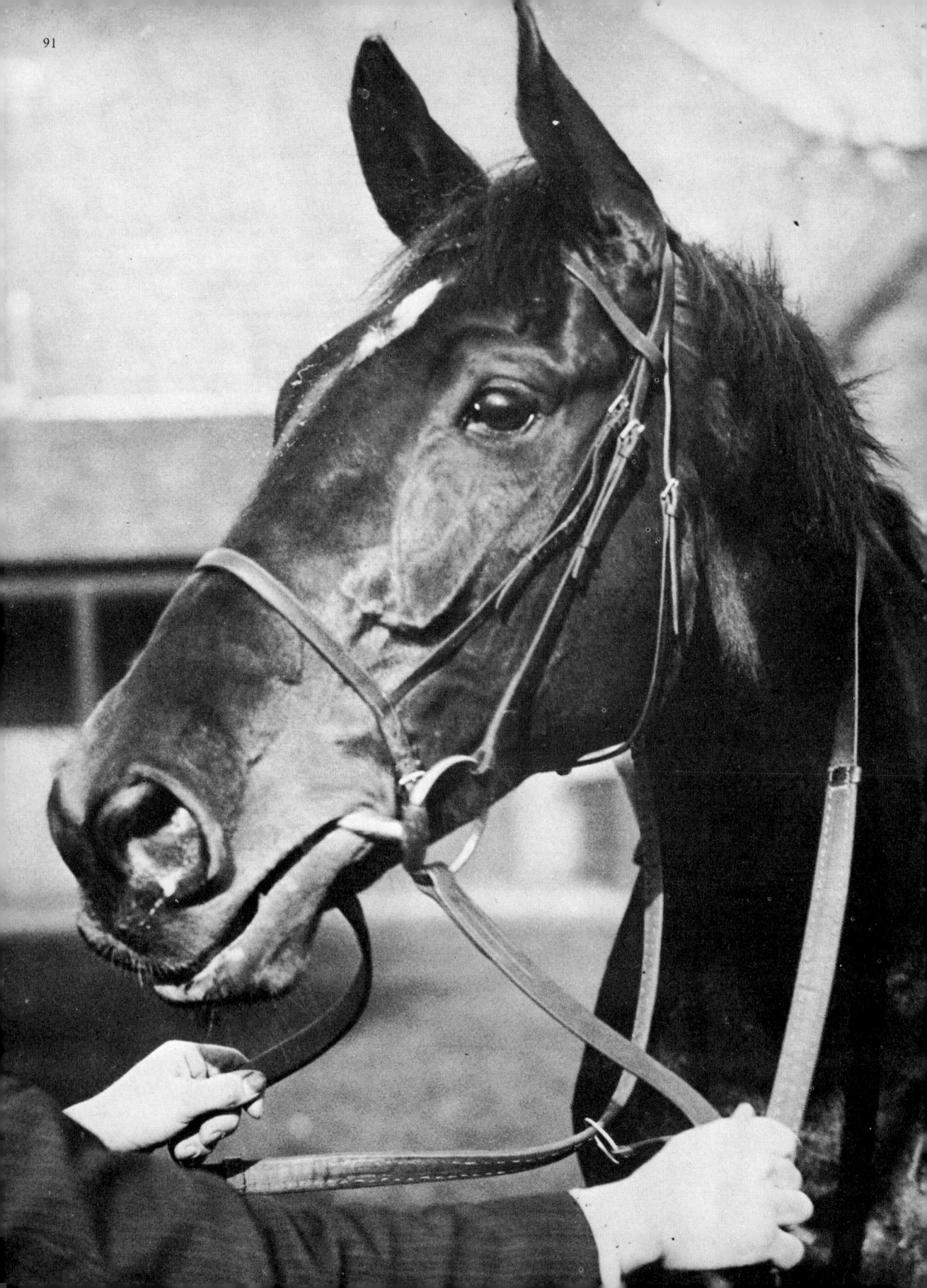

In the early 20th century National Hunt racing was again at a low ebb. The only really valuable races were the National and Sandown's Imperial Cup, a handicap hurdle. This changed in the 1920s with the establishment of Cheltenham's Gold Cup and Champion Hurdle, and with a new generation of rich, sporting owners. The biggest-spending by far was Miss Dorothy Paget, whose incomparable Golden Miller (91 & 92) won five Gold Cups (1932–6) and one National (1934).

4

The National itself remained unique owing to its distance and its gigantic fences (93). It was sometimes won by beautifully-bred horses, such as the little stallion Battleship by the American nonpareil Man O'War, who won the race of 1938 (94).

Although its munificent prize money attracted 'park' champions like Golden Miller, obstacles like Becher's Brook (95) deterred such horses as soon as prizes increased elsewhere. This explains why Arkle (96), three times winner of the Cheltenham Gold Cup and freely compared to Golden Miller, was never subjected to Aintree. But the latter's fascination is still special, and Red Rum (97), only the sixth double winner in history, is a hero at least as popular as Arkle.

98

99

'Fogo' Rowlands's National Hunt Steeplechases were for amateurs riding hunters, but hunt racing of the modern sort did not begin until the 1870s. Then hunts began to put on 'Red Coat Races' for their members, who wore top hats and hunting scarlet; these, and farmers' races, became almost invariable among hunts by 1900. Between the wars farmers, like those at the Duke of Beaufort's point-to-point in 1925 (98), wore bowlers and black or 'ratcatcher'; and ladies, like those of the South and West Wilts (99), often rode races side-saddle. Post-war point-to-points, such as the Cotswold's in 1954 (100), are as festive and sporting as ever, but to the eye sadly resemble ordinary steeplechasing.

5. Jockeys and Trainers

In the 17th century and most of the 18th, horses were ridden by their owners or by nameless boys. The first professional jockey of national reputation was Sam Chifney, whose son, also Sam (101, left) was equally skilful and equally dishonest. His contemporary Jem Robinson (right) was, in sharp contrast, one of the men who made his trade honourable.

12 13 14 15 16 17 18 19 20

The jockey as a great celebrity appeared in the tragic person of Fred Archer (103), brilliant, honest, illiterate, and one of the outstanding personalities of Victorian racing until his suicide, in 1886, at the age of 29. In honesty, as in intuitive understanding of horses, he was compared to Tom Cannon and his three sons, all jockeys (102).

But the sinister precedent of the Chifneys was followed, for all the Jockey Club's authority; in 1887 Charles Wood (104) was in the middle of a racing scandal which resulted in his disgrace and that of an ex-Steward of the Jockey Club. Some 'Gentlemen Riders' were also of odious character: George Baird, 'Mr Abington' (105), liked bullies and trollops, in whose company he died prematurely and squalidly.

106

107

108

15 16 17 18 19 20 21 22

All these men rode with spurs and long leathers, in a style essentially unchanged for 250 years. In 1897 Tod Sloan emerged, under a cloud, from America, and lay along his horse's neck (106). The brothers Lester (109) and Johnny Reiff (108) joined him, also great villains, also great riders. Their 'monkey-on-a-stick' style was detested and derided, but they won so many races that within a couple of seasons every leading English jockey adopted it. Freddy Fox (107) an intelligent man and fine horseman, rode his first winner in 1907 : it never occurred to anybody that he should ride other than like the Americans.

Spy

15 16 17 18 19 20 21 22 23

Of Fox's generation and riding style was Steve Donoghue, whose victory on Captain Cuttle in the 1922 Derby (110) was one of four at Epsom and two wartime substitutes.

Archer, Donoghue and Richards
(112)—Sir Gordon, a successful trainer
and racing manager after he hung up
his boots—are three of the four jockeys
in history who have become
household names. The fourth is Lester
Piggott, no longer champion but
undisputed master, who was spared
none of the miseries when taught by
his father at Lambourn (111).

Since the American, another
influential invasion has been the
Australian; 'Scobie' Breasley (113)
and his countrymen have shown
themselves wonderful, gentle jockeys
for two-year-olds and brilliant judges
of pace.

Even the most successful jockey's life is full of grind and deprivation: not only riding work in the snow, but also getting down to the weight. Fred Archer's fasting and purging contributed to his suicidal despair. Fixed weights formed part of the conditions for races in the 17th century, and scales by the rubbing-house part of the equipment of racecourses. In the 19th century weighing came indoors (115). Tom Cannon has his saddle, but not his bridle, in 1885; he should have his whip too (114). Donoghue has his, to weigh in after a race which he seems to have won (116), and which seems to be at one of the tropical centres where English jockeys spend their winters. The weight problems of steeplechase jockeys (117) are rather less severe.

118

119

121

120

122

Horses were trained until the late 18th century by unremembered grooms. Some of them became famous and respected, but they were still private servants and their methods were primitive. The first eminent public trainer was John Scott of Whitewall, Yorkshire (120), who attracted the richest owners with the best horses, and won 16 St Legers, nine Oaks and six Derbys. Another successful Yorkshireman was John Osborne, first a leading jockey (119), then like his father a formidable trainer: a progression which has often worked, as with Richards and Breasley, but sometimes lamentably failed. Mat Dawson at Newmarket (118) was one of the two outstanding trainers of the late 19th century, and Fred Archer's master and virtual foster-father. The other was John Porter of Kingsclere. In the next period one of the very best was Alec Taylor of Manton (122) whose owners were few, rich and lucky. His stable-yard (121) was no less functional than palatial.

123

125

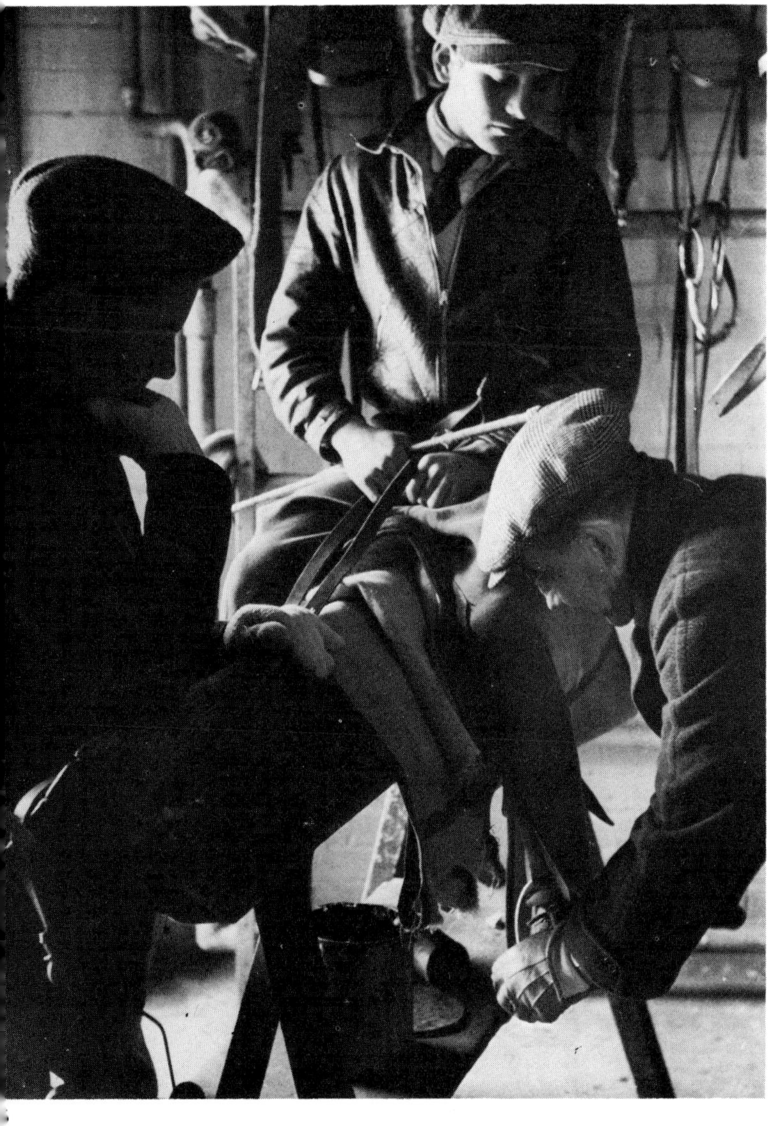

Essentially training is getting each horse perfectly fit by giving it the work and the diet right for its particular needs, and then placing it in the right races. To achieve the first of these, horses are taken out on the gallops, like Sam Darling's string in 1909 (123); and to achieve both first and second the horses are ridden at work by jockeys who can really judge them, like Gordon Richards at Newmarket on one of Noel Murless's (125). Trainers also train their sons and their apprentices, like Keith Piggott (126) with Lester (watching) and the stable-lad on the saddle-horse.

Very busy persons lose some worry, and much fun, by employing racing managers: King Edward VII (right) relied on Lord Marcus Beresford (centre) as well as trainer Richard Marsh and jockey Herbert Jones to achieve Minoru's victory in the 1909 Derby (124).

RACING CALENDAR:

CONTAINING

An ACCOUNT of the

PLATES, MATCHES,

AND

SWEEPSTAKES,

Run for in GREAT-BRITAIN and IRELAND, &c. in the Year 1773.

TOGETHER WITH

An ABSTRACT of all the MATCHES, SWEEPSTAKES, &c. now made, to be run at NEWMARKET, from the CRAVEN MEETING 1774, to the Year 1778.

AND OF

Several MATCHES, &c, made for YORK, BATH, and many other Places.

By JAMES WEATHERBY,

Keeper of the MATCH-BOOK at NEWMARKET.

VOLUME the FIRST.

LONDON:

Printed and Sold by A. GRANT, at SHAKESPEARE'S HEAD, No. 5. Bridges Street, Covent-Garden.

MDCCLXXIII.

127

128

6. Rulers and Rogues

Because so much money was involved, racing needed rules and a court of appeal. These were provided – though hardly outside Newmarket – by Charles II in his lifetime, then by a heavy-gambling, misanthropic Dorset squire called Tregonwell Frampton (129), racing manager to four sovereigns and 'Governor of Newmarket'.

In 1751 the Jockey Club was formed by a group of noblemen and gentlemen. It built premises in Newmarket High Street (130), and within a few years was issuing rules and hearing disputes. It needed records and the publication of its orders; these were provided by various semi-official calendars and, from 1773, by Mr Weatherby's official *Racing Calendar* (127), followed by his *General Stud Book*. Generations of Weatherbys (128) became, and remain, the Civil Service of British racing.

His Royal Highness the Prince of Wales, with

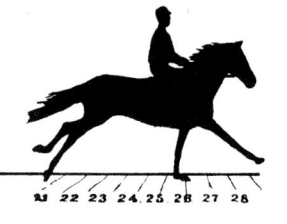

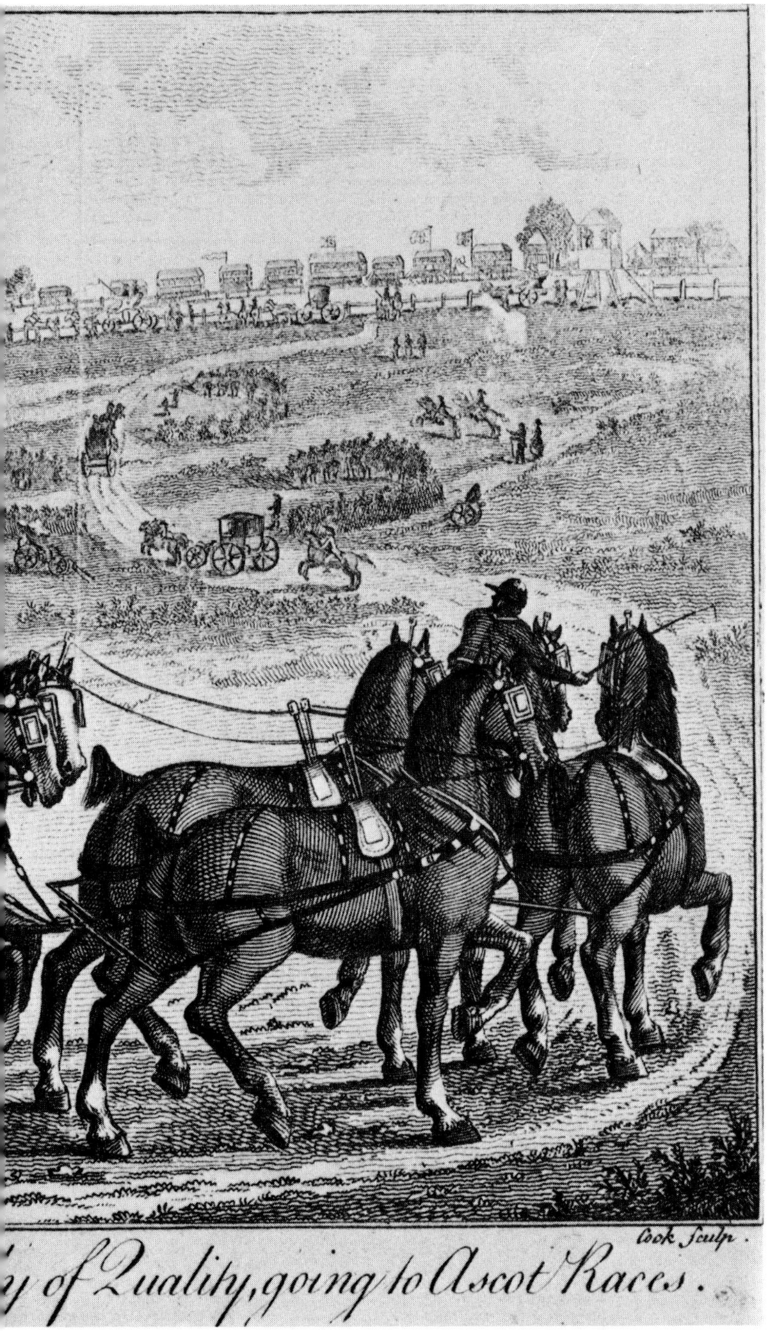
Cook Sculp.
y of Quality, going to Ascot Races.

Equally important to the growth of the Jockey Club's authority was the honesty and courage of Sir Charles Bunbury (132), owner of the first Derby winner Diomed. When he was Senior Steward in 1791, the Club had prestige enough to warn off the turf the Prince of Wales, later George IV (131), after the fraudulent running of a horse called Escape.

132

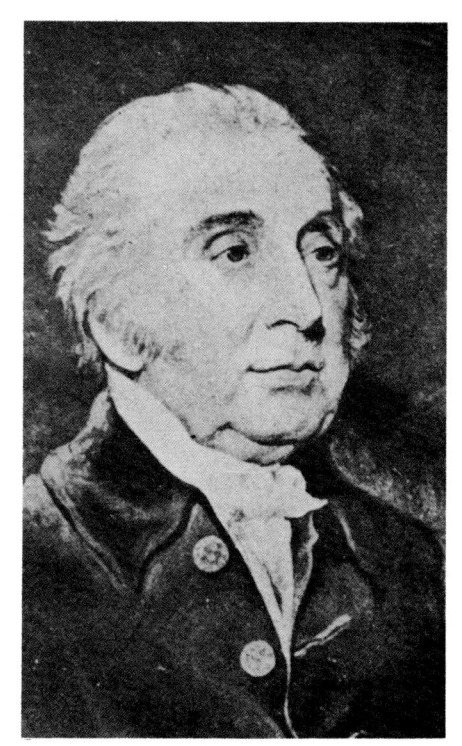

HORSE-VAN.

Though dark and dull this van appears,
  It holds within a *racer* (ray, sir)
Of no slight magnitude, indeed,
  Which will be claimed by *Day*, sir.
Which horse it is of all of those,
  Like ladies' hair in papers,

Is known to none, but all agree
  Outside are many *gapers.*
Strange cavalcade! but stranger st
  Enough to make one smile,
The man that lingers in *the rear*
  Is *van guard* all the while !

134

The fourth racing dictator was Lord George Bentinck (135), who in the 1840s waged violent and successful war on all kinds of villains. His own position was somewhat ambiguous; he was a gigantic plunger, and invented the 'horse-van' (133) in order to bring off a betting coup in the 1836 St Leger. None of this was true of Admiral Rous (134), who handicapped the Voltigeur-Flying Dutchman match, and went on to reform racing's government to such effect that no single dictator was thereafter either possible or necessary.

7

But much in detail was still amiss. Sir John Astley (137) became Chairman of the Jockey Club's Rules Committee in 1875, but there was wide disregard of the Manifesto they promulgated (136). However, his rules of 1879, controlling the activities of jockeys, were a large and vital reform. One rule – that professional jockeys might not have a financial interest in any racehorse – was that which Charles Wood broke, and which broke him.

Behind all the administrators' problems lay money and the scale of betting. Wagers were originally struck entirely between individuals, who met for the purpose at a rendezvous beside the racecourse (138).

London. Publish'd June 9th 1807, by H. Humphrey, 27 St. James's Street.

139

At the beginning of the 19th century the 'blacklegs' or 'pencillers' appeared, who 'made a book' by laying against numbers of horses, at various odds, with all comers (139). This made 'stopping' or 'nobbling' a favourite intensely profitable, and in 1811 the 'legs' even caused the string of a leading trainer to be poisoned, on Newmarket Heath, by a tout called Dawson (140).

DANˡ DAWSON.

Bookmakers at last came under a certain control, and betting with them became respectable and seemly (142). They were allotted specific pitches in various enclosures on the racecourse (141), for which they paid a fee to the course; they were not afraid to advertise their names and addresses, or to wear distinctive and jocular hats (143). Bookmakers nevertheless remained the prime movers of most racing fraud, since no one else habitually profited from the bad running or non-running of a favourite.

145

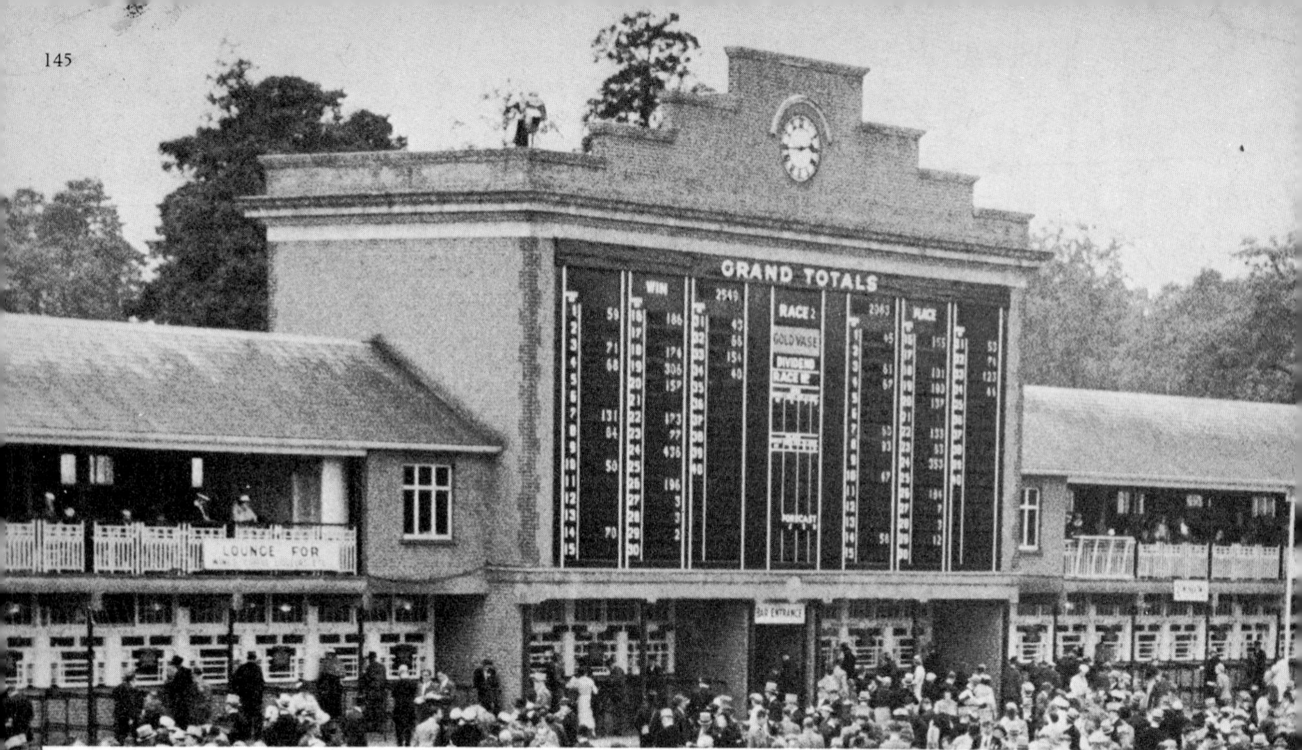
GRAND TOTALS
WIN
RACE 2
GOLD VASE
DIVIDEND
PLACE
LOUNGE FOR
BAR ENTRANCE

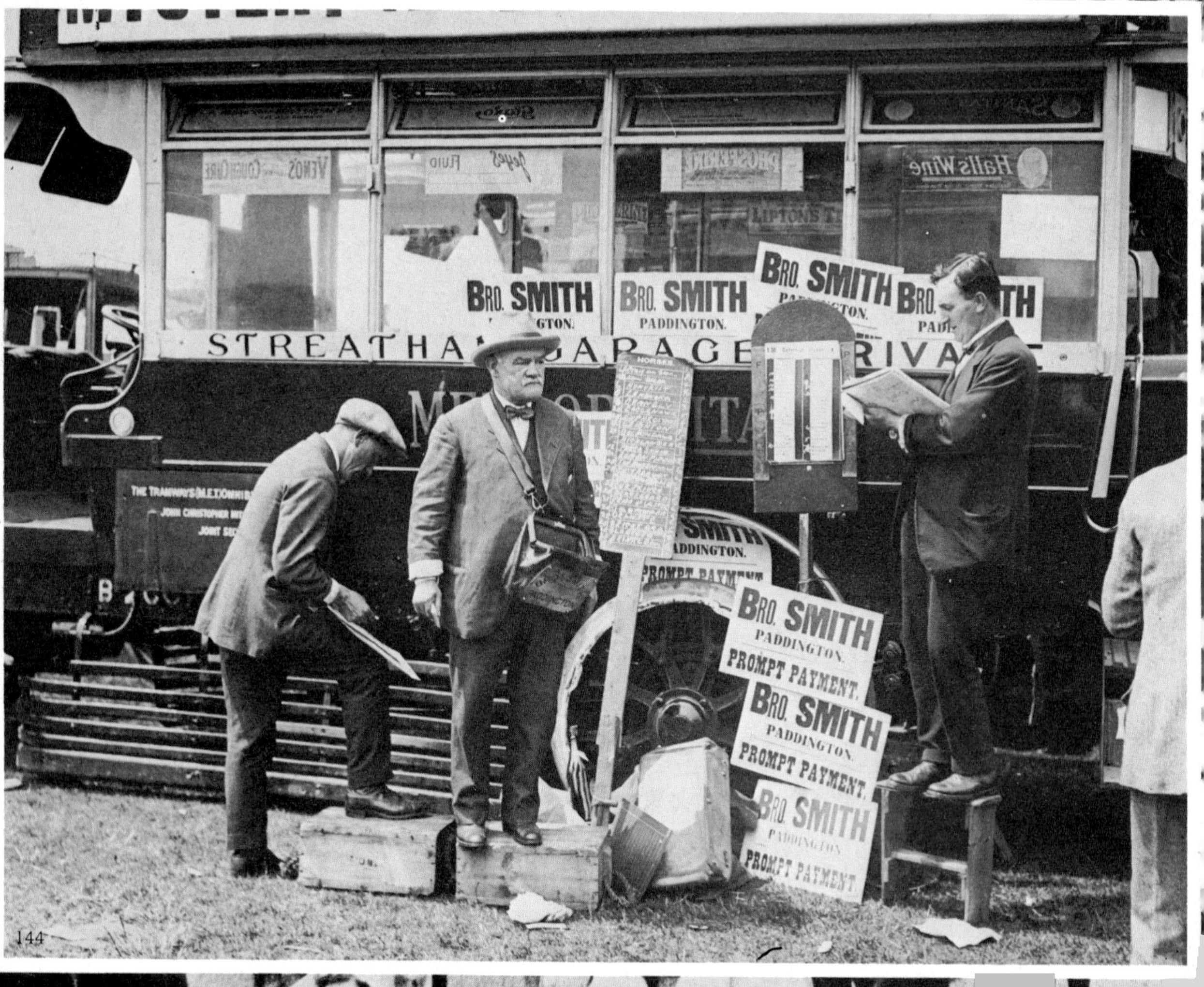
BRO. SMITH
PADDINGTON.
PROMPT PAYMENT.
STREATHAM GARAGE
Halls Wine
VENOS COUGH CURE
Jeyes Fluid
LIPTONS
HORSES

144

26 27 28 29 30 31 32 33 33

Though prompt payment was freely and often truthfully promised (144), defaulters who 'bagged' a horse – took bets about it on which they had no intention of paying out – were a Victorian problem which survived in the 20th-century Welsher (146). The older defaulters were ducked and occasionally lynched; the modern Welsher is protected from violence by arrest. It was partly these problems, partly the need to plough back some betting money into racing, that caused the introduction of the Australian mechanical Totalisator (145). The intention was to transform racing's finance and its probity, but without a statutory Tote monopoly this hope has turned out vain, as most people, and all heavy bettors, prefer dealing with bookies who lay them a price.

146

147

Another effect of the gigantic
volume of betting was the
proliferation of tipsters, who became
a major industry in the 1840s. Some,
like 'Prince Monolulu' (149) between
the wars and for a few years after,
became celebrities without whom no
major meeting was complete. Some
gave good tips – the 'Pearlies' (148)
gave Papyrus for the 1923 Derby, and
it won at the nice if strange odds of
100 to 15. Tipsters appeal to the
get-rich-quick instinct, and when
they can avoid the racecourse police
they still draw good crowds (147).

What would the Godolophin
Arabian have made of such scenes?
Or Grimalkin? Or the Arab, whose
horse-breeding over 1000 years made
the whole extraordinary business
possible? (150).

148

PURE ARABIAN, Presented to HER MAJESTY
by THE IMAUM of Muscat.
(See pp. 29, 123, &c)

THE GODOLPHIN BARB,
Ancestor of the most celebrated Racers on the British Turf.
(See Pages 28, 29, 66, 67, 115, 123, &c &c)

Drawn Expressly for the Book of Field Sports.

London, Henry Lea, 22 Warwick Lane.